A Book of Prayers for Those Who Grieve

This edition copyright © 1995 Lion Publishing

Published by
Lion Publishing plc
Sandy Lane West, Oxford, England
ISBN 0 7459 3356 4
Albatross Books Pty Ltd
PO Box 320, Sutherland, NSW 2232, Australia
ISBN 0 7324 1318 4

First edition 1995
10 9 8 7 6 5 4 3 2 1 0

A catalogue record for this book is available
from the British Library

Printed and bound in Singapore

A BOOK OF PRAYERS
for
Those Who Grieve

Contents

Introduction

The eternal God is our refuge
and underneath are the everlasting arms.

FROM THE BOOK OF DEUTERONOMY

We can be so busy and preoccupied, in the days immediately following the death of a loved one, that the true process of grieving is postponed. Our prayers are immediate and focused on getting through all that has to be done. But the days that follow can be some of the most difficult and challenging we will ever have to live through. These are often the times when prayer – telling all our needs, thoughts and feelings to a loving heavenly Father – is the only resource available to us.

This anthology is designed to provide prayers and insights, not only for the early days, but for the weeks and months that follow. We hope it will become a source of comfort and encouragement — a constant reminder that, however we feel, beneath us are the arms of the eternal, loving God, and his ears are always open to our prayer.

First Shock

Lord God, in the loneliness of my loss
I come to you. I cannot express the
emptiness I feel. Please be near me.
I cannot imagine how I will carry on.
Please support me. I cannot bear the
sorrow. Give me your peace.

Lord – why? What have I done to you
that you could do this to me?
I thought you cared, I thought you were
    good;
Why have you turned against me?
No, don't give me any textbook answers
about the why and how of suffering!
Just – please – give me some sense of
    being held
while the questions are wept and swept
to a stillness within.

KATE COMPSTON

9

The Day of the Funeral

Lord Jesus Christ, I come to you
at the beginning of this day;
in all my loneliness and uncertainty I
    come.
I thank you for all those who will be
    sharing the day with me,
for the minister, relatives and friends,
and all those who have been so helpful.
Help me not to worry about the
    arrangements that have been made,
about the visitors who will be coming,
about my fear of emotion, about the
    service, about the weather.
I bring this day to you; help me in my
    weakness to prove your strength.

CHRISTIAN PUBLICITY ORGANIZATION

We give back to you, O God, those whom you gave to us. You did not lose them when you gave them to us and we do not lose them by their return to you.

Your dear Son has taught us that life is eternal and love cannot die, so death is only an horizon and an horizon is only the limit of our sight. Open our eyes to see more clearly and draw us close to you that we may know that we are nearer to our loved ones, who are with you. You have told us that you are preparing a place for us; prepare us also for that happy place, that where you are we may also be always,

O dear Lord of life and death.

WILLIAM PENN

Father of all, by whose mercy and grace
your saints remain in everlasting light
and peace: we remember with
thanksgiving those whom we love but
see no longer; and we pray that in them
your perfect will may be fulfilled;
through Jesus Christ our Lord.

ALTERNATIVE SERVICE BOOK, 1980

Mourning

He is gone; his pain is over and he is gone. The funeral is over and the family and friends have left. The letters are answered. But the emptiness remains.

The emptiness and so much more. I am angry, God. I am angry at him for dying and angry at you for letting him die. I am angry at friends, who have been so kind, because they are alive and because those they love are alive.

I am angry because I failed him so often. I hurt him. I was selfish, thoughtless, mean. And now he is gone, and I cannot undo the past.

It might be easier to pretend I am not angry but I cannot fool you, God. Help me through this time of anger and pain, of guilt and loss. Help me to live as he – and you – would like me to live.

AVERY BROOKE

At Night

Lord of the night,
Be with me through the hours of
    darkness,
Let all my questions,
Problems, decisions,
Be enveloped in sleep
That through the mystery
Of the sleeping mind
The difficulties of this day
Will be seen to be easier
In the morning light.
Into your hands, O Lord,
I commit my spirit.

FRANK TOPPING

Dear Jesus, as a hen covers her chicks with her wings to keep them safe, do thou this dark night protect us under your golden wings.

PRAYER FROM INDIA

When fear comes, pause . . .
Say what you are afraid of . . .
Feel the fear . . .
Take time . . .
then the barrier to trust will be
    lower,
the jump to be taken no longer
    paralyzing,
Have courage . . .
The Presence is very close and very
    loving.

FROM PRAYER AT NIGHT

Lord, a whole long day of pain now, at
    last is o'er!
Ah, how much we can sustain, I have felt
    once more!
Felt how frail are all our powers, and
    how weak our trust;
If Thou help not, these dark hours crush
    us to the dust.
Could I face the coming night if thou
    wert not near?
Nay, without thy love and might I must
    sink with fear:
Round me falls the evening gloom, sights
    and sounds all cease,
But within his narrow room, night will
    bring no peace!
O Lord, my God, do thou thy holy will!
I will lie still!
I will not stir lest I forsake thine arm,
and break the charm, which lulls me,
    clinging to my Father's breast
in perfect rest!

JOHN KEBLE

Abide with me; fast falls the eventide;
The darkness deepens; Lord with me
    abide!
When other helpers fail, and comforts
    flee,
Help of the helpless, O abide with me.

HENRY FRANCIS LYTE

O Lord Jesus,
Please abide with me.
Dispel my deep loneliness!
No one can be my companion for ever
But you are the Lord who is everywhere
Present at all times
Only you are my dear companion and
saviour.

In the long dark night
Along the silent shadowy pathways
I beg you to grasp my hand.
When others have forgotten me
Please remember me in eternity!
In the name of Jesus. Amen.

DR ANDREW SONG

Lord, all these years we were so close to one another, we did everything together, we seemed to know what each was feeling, without the need of words, and now she is gone. Every memory hurts . . . sometimes there comes a feeling that she is near, just out of sight. Sometimes I feel your reproach that to be so submerged in grief is not to notice that she is as eager to keep in touch with me, as I with her. O dear Lord, I pray out of a sore heart that it may be so, daring to believe that it can be so.

GEORGE APPLETON (1902–93)

Fear of the Future

Please Lord,
Help me to be brave and strong in you
and take my fear away.

STEPHEN MATTHEWS

Set free, O Lord, my soul from all
restlessness and anxiety; give me that
peace and power which flow from you;
keep me in all perplexities and
distresses, in all fears and faithlessness;
that so upheld by your power and stayed
on the rock of your faithfulness, I may
through storm and stress remain in you,
through Jesus Christ our Lord.

FROM NEW EVERY MORNING

Lord,
where tears fall through tragedy or
    heartbreak
enter the silence and hold me tight
lest in bitterness I blame you
or those close to me
when I should be trusting you with those
    I love
and groping my way towards gratitude
for the time I have been privileged to
    share with them.

FROM FURTHER EVERYDAY PRAYERS

O my God, I have no idea where I am going. I do not see the road ahead of me . . . Nor do I really know myself, and the fact that I think I am following your will does not mean that I am actually doing so. But I desire to do your will, and know that the very desire pleases you. Therefore, I will trust you always though I may seem to be lost. I will not fear, for you are always with me, O my dear God.

THOMAS MERTON (1915–68)

As the rain hides the stars,
as the autumn mist hides the hills,
as the clouds veil the blue of the sky,
so the dark happenings of my lot
hide the shining of your face from
    me.
Yet, if I may hold your hand in the
    darkness,
it is enough.
Since I know that,
though I may stumble in my going,
you do not fall.

GAELIC PRAYER,
translated by Alistair MacLean

O God,
I cannot begin this day without
    thee.
I cannot trust myself.
Help me,
that I may know that
I am not alone.

H.C. ALLEMAN

Strength to Carry On

Ah Lord, my prayers are dead, my affections dead and my heart is dead; but you are a living God and I bear myself upon you.

WILLIAM BRIDGE (1600–70)

Support us, Lord, when we are silent through grief! Comfort us when we are bent down with sorrow! Help us as we bear the weight of our loss! Lord, our Rock and our Redeemer, give us strength!

JEWISH FUNERAL SERVICE

Give me the strength for this day
to weep when I should weep
to accept the comfort that memories
    bring
to face decisions with courage
to meet people
    those who love me
    those who want to help me
    those who want to comfort me
    but don't know what to say
Thank you for them all.

I said to the man who stood at the Gate
of the Year, 'Give me a light that I may
tread safely into the unknown.' And he
replied, 'Go out into the darkness and
put your hand into the hand of God. That
shall be to you better than light and safer
than a known way!'

MINNIE LOUISE HASKINS

It's me, it's me, it's me, O Lord,
Standin' in the need of prayer.
Not my brother, not my sister,
But it's me, O Lord,
Standin' in the need of prayer.

NEGRO SPIRITUAL

In the shadow of your wings I find
    protection.
O Lord, the giver of life,
I thank you for the love I have known,
    for joys and sorrows shared.
I accept, Lord, that you have taken the
    life that you once gave.
Please bring your gentle healing to the
    hurt that comes with parting.
Thank you, lord Jesus, that you care
    about me.

CHRISTIAN PUBLICITY ORGANIZATION

Lead, kindly light, amid the encircling
    gloom,
Lead thou me on;
The night is dark, and I am far from
    home;
Lead thou me on.
Keep thou my feet; I do not ask to see
The distant scene; one step enough for
    me.

I was not ever thus, nor prayed that thou
Shouldst lead me on;
I loved to choose and see my path; but
    now
Lead thou me on.
I loved the garish day, and spite of fears,
Pride ruled my will: remember not past
    years.

So long thy power has blest me, sure it
  still
Will lead me on,
O'er moor and fen, o'er crag and
  torrent, till
The night is gone,
And with the morn those angel faces
  smile,
Which I have loved long since, and lost
  awhile.

JOHN HENRY NEWMAN (1801–90)

We are weak: out of weakness make us
   strong.
We are in peril of death: come and heal
   us.
We believe: help thou our unbelief.
We hope: let us not be disappointed of
   our hope.
We love: grant us to love much,
to love ever more and more,
to love all,
and most of all to love you.

CHRISTINA ROSSETTI

O Lord, hold my hand while I run this
    race.
O Lord, hold my hand while I run this
    race.
O Lord, hold my hand while I run this
    race
for I don't want to run this race in vain.

Let me do my work each day; and if the darkened hours of despair overcome me, may I not forget the strength that comforted me in the desolation of other times.

May I still remember the bright hours that found me walking over the silent hills of my childhood, or dreaming, on the margin of the quiet river, when a light glowed within me, and I promised my early God to have courage amidst the tempests of the changing years. Spare me from bitterness and from the sharp passions of unguarded moments. May I not forget that poverty and riches are of the spirit. Though the world know me not, may my thoughts and actions be such as shall keep me friendly with myself.

Lift my eyes from the earth, and let me not forget the uses of the stars. Forbid that I should judge others lest I condemn myself. Let me not follow the clamour of the world, but walk calmly in my path.

Give me a few friends who will love me for what I am; and keep burning before my vagrant steps the kindly light of hope. And though age and infirmity overtake me, and I come not within sight of the castle of my dreams, teach me still to be thankful for life and for time's olden memories that are good and sweet; and may the evening's twilight find me gentle still.

MAX EHRMANN

Finding Peace and Hope

O Lord, the giver of all life,
I thank you for the love I have known,
for joys and sorrows shared.
I accept, Lord, that you have taken the
    life that you once gave.
Please bring your gentle healing to the
    hurt that comes with parting.
Thank you, Lord Jesus, that you care
    about me. Amen.

CHRISTIAN PUBLICITY ORGANIZATION

We seem to give them back to you, O God, who gave them to us . . . Yet as you did not lose them in giving, so we do not lose them by their return. O lover of souls, you do not give as the world gives. What you give you do not take away; for what is yours is ours also if we are yours. And life is eternal and love is immortal; and death is only a horizon; and a horizon is nothing save the limit of our sight. Lift us up, strong son of God, that we may see further; cleanse our eyes that we may see more clearly; draw us closer to yourself that we may know ourselves to be nearer to our loved ones who are with you. And while you prepare a place for them, prepare us also for that happy place, that where you are we may also be for evermore. Amen

CHARLES HENRY BRENT (1862–1929)

O Lord, my God! The amazing horrors of darkness were gathered round me, and covered me all over, and I saw no way to go forth; I felt the depth and extent of the misery of my fellow-creatures separated from the divine harmony, and it was heavier than I could bear; and I was crushed down under it; I lifted up my hand, I stretched out my arm, but there was none to help me; I looked round about, and was amazed. In the depths of misery, O Lord, I remembered that you are omnipotent; that I had called you Father; and I felt that I loved you, and I as made quiet in my will, and I waited for deliverance from you. You had pity on me, when no man could help me; I saw that meekness under suffering was showed to us in the most affecting example of your Son, and

you taught me to follow him, and I said,
'Thy will, O Father, be done!'
O Lord our God, from whom neither
life nor death can separate those who
trust in thy love, and whose love holds in
its embrace thy children in this world
and the next; so unite us to thyself that
in fellowship with thee we may always
be united to our loved ones whether
here or there; give us courage,
constancy and hope; through him who
died and was buried and rose again for
us, Jesus Christ our Lord.

WILLIAM TEMPLE (1881–1944)

O Father of all, we pray to thee for those whom we love, but see no longer. Grant them thy peace; let light perpetual shine upon them; and in thy loving wisdom and almighty power work in them the good purpose of thy perfect will; through Jesus Christ our Lord.

For Others Who Grieve

Grant, O Lord, to all those who are
bearing pain, thy spirit of healing, thy
spirit of life, thy spirit of peace and
hope, of courage and endurance. Cast
out from them the spirit of anxiety and
fear; grant them perfect confidence and
trust in thee, that in thy light they may
see light, through Jesus Christ our Lord.

ANON

Watch thou, O Lord, with those who wake, or watch, or weep tonight, and give thine angels charge over those who sleep. Tend thy sick ones, O Lord Christ; rest thy weary ones; bless thy dying ones; soothe thy suffering ones; pity thine afflicted ones; shield thy joyous ones, and all for thy love's sake.

AUGUSTINE OF HIPPO (354–430)

Words from the Bible

Be merciful to me, O God, be merciful,
because I come to you for safety.
In the shadow of your wings I find
    protection
until the raging storms are over.

FROM PSALM 57

Be still and know that I am God

FROM PSALM 46

The Lord is my shepherd,
    I shall not want.
He makes me lie down in green pastures;
    he leads me beside still waters;
    he restores my soul.
He leads me in right paths for his name's
    sake.
Even though I walk through the darkest
    valley,
    I fear no evil;
    for you are with me;
your rod and your staff – they comfort
    me.

You prepare a table before me
   in the presence of my enemies;
You anoint my head with oil;
   my cup overflows.
Surely goodness and mercy shall follow
   me all the days of my life,
And I shall dwell in the house of the Lord
   my whole life long.

PSALM 23

To every thing there is a season,
and a time to every purpose under the
   heaven:
a time to be born, and a time to die;
a time to plant, and a time to pluck up
   that which is planted;
a time to kill, and a time to heal;
a time to break down, and a time to
   build up.

A time to weep, and a time to laugh;
a time to mourn and a time to dance;
a time to cast away stones, and a time to
   gather stones together;
a time to embrace, and a time to refrain
   from embracing.

A time to get, and a time to lose;
a time to keep, and a time to cast away;
a time to rend, and a time to sew;
a time to keep silence, and a time to
  speak.

A time to love, and a time to hate;
a time of war, and a time of peace.

FROM THE BOOK OF ECCLESIASTES

For I am convinced that neither death, nor life, nor angels, nor rulers, nor things present, nor things to come, nor powers, nor height, nor depth, nor anything else in all creation, will be able to separate us from the love of God in Christ Jesus our Lord.

FROM THE BOOK OF ROMANS

The Lord is my light and my salvation;
I will fear no one.
The Lord protects me from all danger;
I will never be afraid.

FROM PSALM 27

God shall wipe away all tears from their
eyes, and there shall be no more death,
neither sorrow, nor crying, neither shall
there be any more pain; for the former
things are passed away.

FROM THE REVELATION OF JOHN

Out of the depths I cry to you,
O Lord;
O Lord, hear my voice.

FROM PSALM 130

Jesus said, 'I am the resurrection and the life. Whoever believes in me will live, even though he dies; and whoever lives and believes in me will never die.'

FROM THE GOSPEL OF JOHN

But now, this is what the Lord says —
he who created you. . .
he who formed you. . .
'Fear not, for I have redeemed you
I have summoned you by name;
you are mine.
When you pass through the waters,
I will be with you;
and when you pass through the rivers,
they will not sweep over you. . .
I am making a way in the desert
and streams in the wasteland.'

FROM THE BOOK OF ISAIAH

As a father is kind to his children,
   so the Lord is kind to those who
   honour him.
He knows what we are made of;
   he remembers that we are dust.

As for us, our life is like grass.
We grow and flourish like a wild flower;
   then the wind blows on it, and it is
   gone –
   no one sees it again.
But for those who honour the Lord, his
   love lasts for ever.

FROM PSALM 103

This I call to mind and
therefore I have hope;
Because of the Lord's great love we are
not consumed,
for his compassions
never fail.
They are new every morning;
great is your faithfulness.

FROM THE BOOK OF LAMENTATIONS

Set me as a seal upon thine heart,
as a seal upon thine arm:
for love is strong as death.

FROM THE SONG OF SONGS

For Reflection

Love is not changed by death,
and nothing is lost
and all in the end is harvest.

EDITH SITWELL

. . . in the very deepest despair there is
hope, and when by grief the entire
universe is suddenly emptied there is
God.

DOUGLAS GRESHAM

Let nothing disturb you, nothing
    alarm you:
while all things fade away
God is unchanging.
Be patient
and you will gain everything:
for with God in your heart
nothing is lacking,
God meets your every need.

TERESA OF AVILA

God's promise of
resurrection is written
not only in books
but in every springtime leaf.

MARTIN LUTHER

The river of death runs through the church of God and at present we cannot see across it; but it is all one church each side, just as London each side of the Thames is all one city. The living and the dead are one 'in Christ'; and we can speak of them to him.

HERBERT TOMKINSON

And these words, 'You will not be overcome,' were said very insistently and strongly, for certainty and strength against every tribulation which may come. He did not say, 'You will not be troubled, you will not be belaboured, you will not be disquieted'; but he said: 'You will not be overcome.' God wants us to pay attention to these words, and always to be strong in faith and trust, in well-being and in woe, for he loves us and delights in us, and so he wishes us to love him and delight in him and trust greatly in him, and all will be well.

JULIAN OF NORWICH

Blessings

We commend unto you, O Lord,
our souls and our bodies,
our minds and our thoughts,
our prayers and our hopes,
our health and our work,
our life and our death,
our parents and brothers and sisters,
our benefactors and friends,
our neighbours, our countrymen,
and all Christian folk,
this day and always.

LANCELOT ANDREWES (1555–1626)

The blessing of the Lord rest and remain upon all his people, in every land, of every tongue; the Lord meet in mercy all that seek him; the Lord comfort all who suffer and mourn; the Lord hasten his coming, and give us, his people, the blessing of peace.

HANDLEY MOULE (1841–1920)

Deep peace of the running wave to you
Deep peace of the flowing air to you
Deep peace of the quiet earth to you
Deep peace of the shining stars to you
Deep peace of the Son of peace to you.

IONA COMMUNITY PRAYER

The Lord bless you, and keep you:
the Lord make his face to shine upon
you, and be gracious unto you:
the Lord lift up the light of his
countenance upon you,
and give you peace.

FROM THE BOOK OF NUMBERS

May the road rise to meet you,
May the wind be always at your back,
May the sun shine warm upon your face,
May the rains fall softly upon your fields.
Until we meet again,
May God hold you in the hollow of his
    hand.

GAELIC PRAYER

Be thou a bright flame before me,
Be thou a guiding star above me,
Be thou a smooth path below me,
Be thou a kindly shepherd behind me
Today, tonight and for ever.

ST COLUMBA (521–527)

May the everlasting Father himself
    take you
in his own generous clasp,
in his own generous arm.

CELTIC PRAYER

May God shield me,
May God fill me,
May God keep me,
May God watch me,
May God bring me
To the land of peace,
To the country of the King,
To the peace of eternity.

God the Father bless me,
Christ guard me,
the Holy Spirit enlighten me,
all the days of my life.
The Lord be the defender and guardian
of my soul and my body, now and ever,
and world without end.

FROM THE BOOK OF CERNE

Acknowledgments

Every attempt has been made to trace copyright holders
of individual prayers. If there have been any inadvertant
omissions in the acknowledgments we apologize to those
concerned.

Darton, Longman and Todd for 'Lord, all these years we were so close'
by George Appleton from *Prayers from a Troubled Heart*;

HarperCollins Publishers Ltd for 'He is gone;' by Avery Brooke
from *Plain Prayers for a Complicated World*;

BBC Publications for material from *New Every Morning*;

Christian Publicity Organization;

National Christian Education Council for material from
Further Everday Prayers.